The Funcraft Book of Print and Paint

SCHOLASTIC BOOK SERVICES
NEW YORK · TORONTO · LONDON · AUCKLAND · SYDNEY · TOKYO

Written and devised by:
Heather Amery and Anne Civardi
Assisted by:
Jim Corless

Designed by:
Sally Burrough
Illustrated by:
Malcolm English
Additional prints by:
Jim Corless

Published by Scholastic Book Services,
a division of Scholastic Magazines, Inc.
by arrangement with
Ottenheimer Publishers, Inc.

Manufactured in the
United States of America

Scholastic ISBN—0-590-11935-4

Scholastic Book Services
An Usborne Book
One of the Scholastic FunCraft Series

About this Book

This book shows you how to print patterns and pictures in all kinds of different ways on paper, cardboard and cloth. You will need poster paints, colored inks and fabric dyes. There is a list on page 4 to tell you what to ask for and where to buy it. You can probably find sheets of paper, cardboard and brushes at home.

At the end of the book there are ways to frame and hang pictures. There are also lots of ideas for using your prints.

The patterns and pictures in this book show you just a few of the marvelous things you can do with prints and paint. Try inventing your own, using as many colors as you like.

The Funcraft Book of Print and Paint

Contents

Before You Start

These are the things you need to make the prints in this book:

Paint - powder or poster paints are good for printing.

Paper - use drawing paper for the best prints. Practice printing on rough paper. Try using rolls of white shelf paper, wall lining paper or the back of a roll of old wallpaper. Some art shops sell sheets of thick, cheap paper.

Colored cardboard - for picture frames. Stationery and art shops sell sheets of brightly colored cardboard.

Waterproof inks - They are sold in stationery and art shops.

Fabric Paints - ask in art or craft shops for fabric or textile paints.

Expanded polystyrene - this white, light plastic material is often used for packing breakable things. Use thick pieces for printing blocks.

Sheet sponge - use this artificial foam sponge to dab on paint and to make sponge rollers.

Paste - for paint and paste prints, use paper glue or all purpose glue.

Glue - use an all-purpose glue for sticking cardboard and sponge rollers.

Black India ink - this is sold by stationery and art shops.

Stencil brush - buy this in a stationery or art shop.

Water-based block printing colors - these are good for monoprints.

Getting Ready

Printing and painting can be a messy business, so it is a good idea to get everything ready before you start. Cover a table or bench with lots of newspaper and put it over any furniture which could be splashed with paint. If you are making very long prints on rolls of paper, put newspaper on the floor and use it as a working surface. Wear old clothes or something over your clothes. An old shirt makes a good painting smock.

Collect all the things you will need for one kind of printing and have them ready to use. Rags are useful for wiping paint off your hands and mopping up spilled paint or ink. When you have made a print, hang it up or lay it down flat to dry. On pages 44, 45 and 46 there are lots of things to make with your prints. Remember to clean up when you have finished printing. Put the tops on bottles and tubes of paint and wash the brushes.

1 Making a Dabber

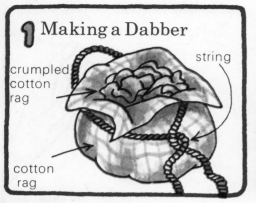

crumpled cotton rag

string

cotton rag

Crumple up a small piece of cotton rag into a ball. Put it in the middle of a small square of rag and tie with string, like this.

2

Dip the dabber in some paint and use it to cover printing blocks evenly with paint or to spread the paint on a tray for monoprints.

Brushes

wipe with rag

When you have finished with a brush, wash it in clean water and dry the bristles with a rag, wiping from the handles to the tip. Store brushes standing on the handles.

Printing Base

When you print with vegetables, leaves or with blocks, put a thick wad of newspaper under the printing paper. This will help you to make good, clear prints.

1 Making a Print Pad

Cut a square of old, thick cotton or wool cloth. Put it on a flat plate and pour on some paint. Press printing blocks and vegetables on the pad to cover them with paint.

2

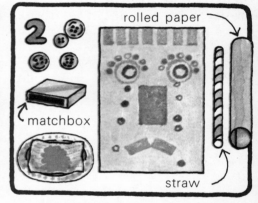

rolled paper

matchbox

straw

Try using the pad for putting paint on such things as matchboxes, straws, buttons, erasers, rolled-up paper and printing with them. Make up a pattern or a picture.

Paper Stretching

When paper gets very wet with water or paint, it sometimes dries in wrinkles. Try this way of stretching paper before you use it for printing, for Paste and Paint Pictures and for Wash-Off Pictures. The paper will then dry flat.

1

board

paper

wet sponge

Put a sheet of paper down on a board or old table top. Rub it gently all over with a clean sponge dipped in clean water.

2

wet paper

strips

Wet four strips of gummed paper tape, a little longer than the paper. Press them down on the edges of the paper, sticking it to the board or table. Leave to dry. Pull off strips.

Finger, Thumb and Hand Prints

The secret of making good fingerprints is to use paint that is not too wet, just sticky. Spread some poster paint on an old tray or plate, or use a print pad (see page 5). Dab your fingers in the paint and press them gently onto a clean sheet of paper. If the paint stickiness is just right, it will show up the swirls of tiny lines on your fingertips.

To print bigger shapes, spread paint on a tray or plate. Press down your fists, palms or the sides of your hands and roll backward and forward to cover them with paint. When the prints are dry, draw or paint in details to make pictures.

With a magnifying glass you can see that the lines on your fingertips are really grooves and ridges.

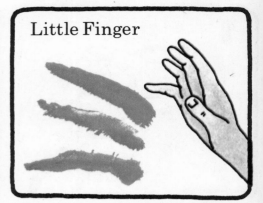

Little Finger

Curl your little finger and rock it toward the tip as you press it down.

leaves
(little finger)

trunk
(side of hand)

cavemen
(rolling forefingers)

cavemen
(forefingers)

legs
(rolling fist)

Rolling Thumb

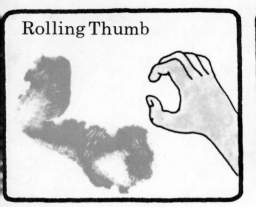

Press down your thumb, and rock it slightly toward the knuckle.

Rolling Fist

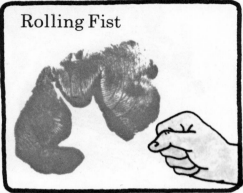

Make a fist and press it down with a rolling movement.

Side of Hand

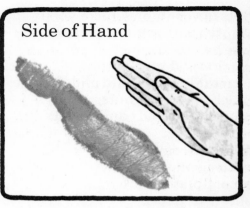

Press down the side of your hand and rock it from side to side.

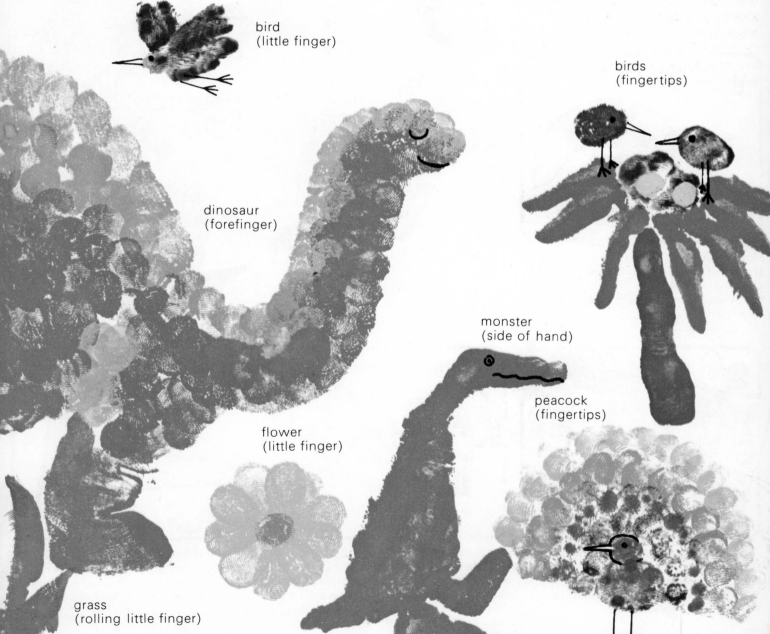

bird
(little finger)

birds
(fingertips)

dinosaur
(forefinger)

monster
(side of hand)

peacock
(fingertips)

flower
(little finger)

grass
(rolling little finger)

Vegetable Prints

Lots of vegetables make good printed patterns and pictures. Use hard ones, such as potatoes, carrots and turnips, or vegetables with hard middles, like Brussels sprouts, mushrooms and cauliflowers.

You will need
poster paint
an old plate or a baking tray
sheets of paper
a table knife
a pair of scissors for making
  holes
lots of different vegetables
a paintbrush

1 Making a Print

press in paint

Pour a little paint onto a plate or tray and spread it out with a brush. Dip the cut side of a vegetable in the paint and then press it onto a sheet of paper.

radish crowd

carrot goal posts

parsley grass

2

Try practicing a print on scrap paper first. If the vegetable is dry, the paint should be wet, but if the vegetable is very juicy, make the paint much thicker.

Cutting Vegetables

radish

celery

cauliflower

carrot

Cut some vegetables in half to make printing shapes. To cut a vegetable, always hold it down on a hard, flat surface and cut down with a knife.

Make different prints from the same vegetable by cutting it in different ways. Cut one onion lengthwise and another one across and see what patterns they print.

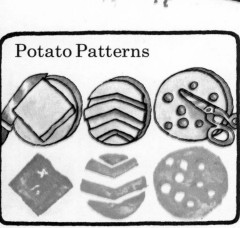

potato ball

cauliflower tree

carrot branches

celery hair

potato face

mushroom jersey

potato trousers

carrot boots

Carrot Stars

Make carrot stars or flowers by slicing off the end of a large carrot. Then cut out little triangles all around the edge of the slice with a table knife.

Onion Flowers

carrot leaves

Cut an onion in half to print flower petals. Use four or more onion prints to make a flower, like this. Use a sliced carrot to print leaves.

Potato Patterns

Potato Roller

roll

scoop out holes

Slice the end off a potato and cut shapes in the flat surface with a table knife, like this. To make potato spot prints, scoop out holes with closed scissors.

Scoop holes in a smooth, round potato with the ends of closed scissors. Push two pencils halfway through the potato to make handles, like this.

Hold the pencil handles and roll the potato in poster paint and then across a sheet of paper. This is a good way to make a border or to decorate notepaper.

Leaf Prints

Collect lots of green leaves or ferns and try printing with them. Get as many different shapes and sizes as you can and use both sides of each leaf to make different patterns.

You will need
leaves of different shapes and
    sizes
thick poster paint
a plate or old baking tray
sheets of paper
thin cardboard
a paint brush

1 How to Take Prints

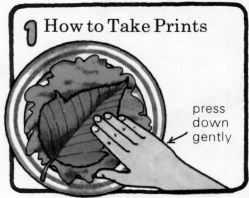

press down gently

Spread some thick poster paint on a plate or baking tray. Lay a leaf on the paint and press it down gently to coat it with paint.

2

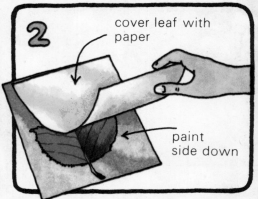

cover leaf with paper

paint side down

Pick up the leaf and put it, paint side down, on a piece of paper. Cover it with another sheet of paper and rub it gently all over with the side of your hand.

Leaf Hills

brush on paint

Use long, broad leaves, such as iris leaves, to print hills and grass. Brush thick paint on one side and print it across the paper.

Leaf and Fern Trees

Try making leaf and fern prints look like trees and bushes. Use leaves of different shapes and sizes and print with as many colors as you like.

Colored Trees

Try printing leaf trees in several colors. Brush two or three colors on different parts of a leaf and press it down on a sheet of paper.

Leaf Pictures

Use lots of leaf prints to make patterns and pictures. Try printing flowers, birds with leaf wings or sailing boats. Draw or paint the flower stems or bird heads.

For Christmas cards, print a fern on the outside of a folded piece of cardboard. When the print is dry, paint in snow, packages and candles.

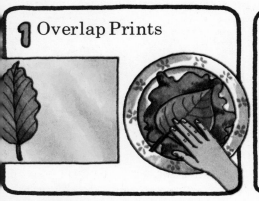

1 Overlap Prints

To make printed leaves look as if they are behind one another, press a leaf onto some paint. Put it down gently on a sheet of paper.

2

Press a second leaf in the paint and put it on the paper so it overlaps the first one. Try putting down a third leaf in a different color.

3 lift up leaves

Put a sheet of paper over the three leaves and rub it gently all over. Pick up the top sheet and lift off the leaves, one by one, without smudging the paint.

Mirror Prints

These prints are called mirror prints because the two shapes on either side of the folded paper are exactly the same, like the reflection in a mirror. They are quick and easy to make and every one is different.

You will need
thick poster paint
sheets of paper
pieces of string for string
  prints
a paintbrush
an old plate
newspaper

1 Mystery Blob Prints

newspaper

Fold a piece of paper in half. Open it and drop or flick big blobs of wet poster paint onto one side, near the fold. Use lots of different colors, like this.

Mystery Blob

2 fold paper over · press and rub

Fold over the paper so that the clean half touches the paint. Rub the paper hard all over with your hand.

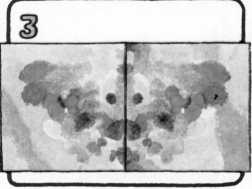

3

Try making lots of blob prints, in different shapes, using lots of colors, like this.

Painted Print

1 Painted Prints

Fold a piece of paper in half. Open it and paint a shape or pattern on one side of the paper, near the fold. Use paint that is not too wet.

2

paint in leaves

Fold the paper over and rub all over it with the side of your hand. Open the paper and draw or paint in details to make a picture.

1 String Pull Prints

string

Put some thick poster paint on an old plate. Dip a piece of thin string in the paint and brush the paint over it to cover it with paint.

2

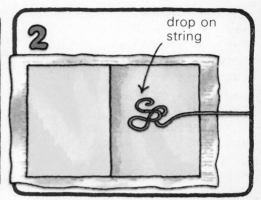

drop on string

Fold a sheet of paper in half. Open it out and drop the painted string onto one side of the paper, leaving one end of the string hanging over the edge of the paper.

3

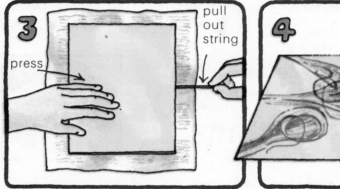

press

pull out string

Fold over the paper and hold it down with one hand. Pull out the string hanging over the edge of the paper with the other hand. Now open out the paper.

4

Try dropping lots of pieces of string, each dipped in a different colored paint, onto the paper. Hold down the folded paper and pull out all the strings at the same time.

1 String Drop Prints

drop string on paper

Dip a piece of string in some paint, making sure it is well covered. Drop the string on one side of a folded sheet of paper. Fold over the paper and press hard on it.

2

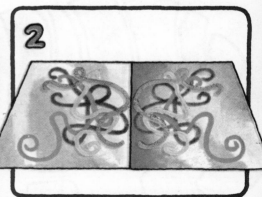

Open up the paper and pick up the string. Let the print dry. Do the same again using a different color paint. Do it lots of times until you have a really colorful print.

Glue and Powder Prints

You will need
sugar, dry sand, or salt
dry powder paints or powder
  dyes
glue or paste
scissors
sheets of paper
a paint brush
old bowls for mixing colors
thin cardboard
old newspaper

1 Glue Painting

Draw a shape, perhaps an elephant or a monster, on a piece of paper. Paint glue over the parts you want colored, either all over or in stripes or dots.

2

Mix up some sugar, sand or salt with one color of powder paint or dye. Sprinkle the mixture over the glue shape, making sure that it is well covered.

Fern and Glue Print

1 Glue Print Pictures

Cut a shape out of cardboard. Paint one side with glue and press it, glue side down, onto some paper. Lift the shape up quickly so that it does not have time to stick.

2

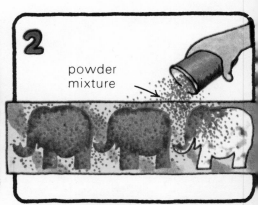

Sprinkle a sugar and powder paint mixture onto the paper and then shake it off gently. Do this lots of times until you have a row of glue prints, like this.

Glue Painting

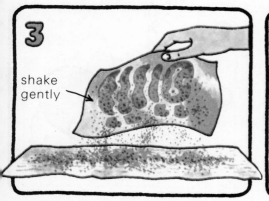

3

shake gently

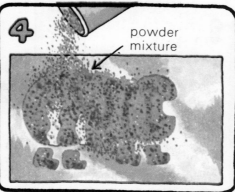

4

powder mixture

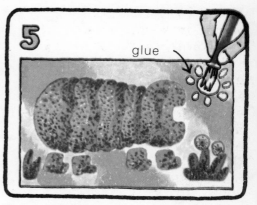

5

glue

Pick up the paper and shake it gently over some newspaper. A lot of the colored sugar, sand or salt will stick to the glue and leave a colored shape.

If you want to put another color on the glue shape, paint the uncolored parts with glue and sprinkle on a different colored mixture. Shake it off gently.

Decorate the picture by painting more shapes with glue and sprinkle on more colors, one at a time. You can use the mixture left on the newspaper again.

Leaf and Glue Print

Leaf and Glue Prints

Use leaves or ferns to make prints. Cover one side of the leaf with glue, press it down on paper, lift it off and sprinkle a sugar and paint mixture over the glue print.

Homemade Colors

You can use kitchen powders like cocoa, instant coffee, paprika, ground red chilli powder, mustard powder and blue detergent powder instead of powder paint or dye.

Roller Prints

You will need

a cardboard tube about 2¾ in.
  long
a small piece of cardboard
two pencils
a sheet of foam sponge (see
  page 4)
strong all purpose glue
a knitting needle
an empty thread spool
some art eraser or non-hardening
  clay
poster paint
an old baking tray
sheets of paper
scissors

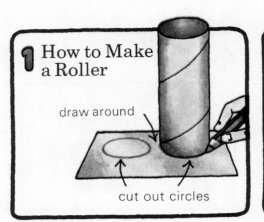

1 How to Make a Roller

draw around

cut out circles

Draw two circles on some
cardboard, using the end of the
cardboard tube as a guide, like this.
Cut out the circles with scissors.

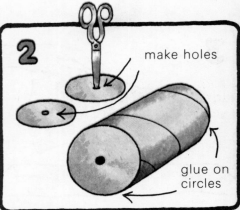

2

make holes

glue on
circles

Make a hole in the center of each
cardboard circle with scissors, like
this. Glue the circles to the two
ends of the tube with strong glue
and leave the glue to dry.

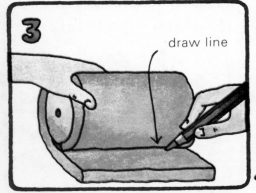

3

draw line

Cut a piece of sheet sponge the same
length as the tube. Put the tube on
the sponge and roll it up, like this.
Draw a line along the edge and cut
along the line.

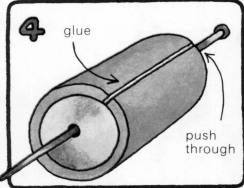

4

glue

push
through

Roll the sponge around the tube and
glue the edges together. Do not
glue the sponge to the roller. Leave
it to dry. Push a knitting needle
through the tube, like this.

5

roll

Spread paint on an old baking tray.
Roll the paint out with the sponge
roller until the roller is evenly
coated with paint.

6

roll across paper

Put a piece of paper on top of some
newspaper and push the roller
across the paper, like this. You can
use the roller to color in part of a
picture like the sky, sea or grass.

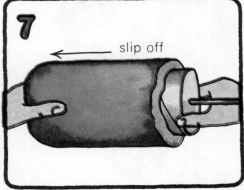

7

slip off

To clean the sponge, slip it off the
cardboard tube and wash the paint
off with soap and water. Leave it
to dry and then slide it back onto
the tube.

Sponge Cut-Outs

cut out
shapes

You can print lots of different
patterns by cutting shapes out of
the sponge on the roller with a
pair of scissors, like this.

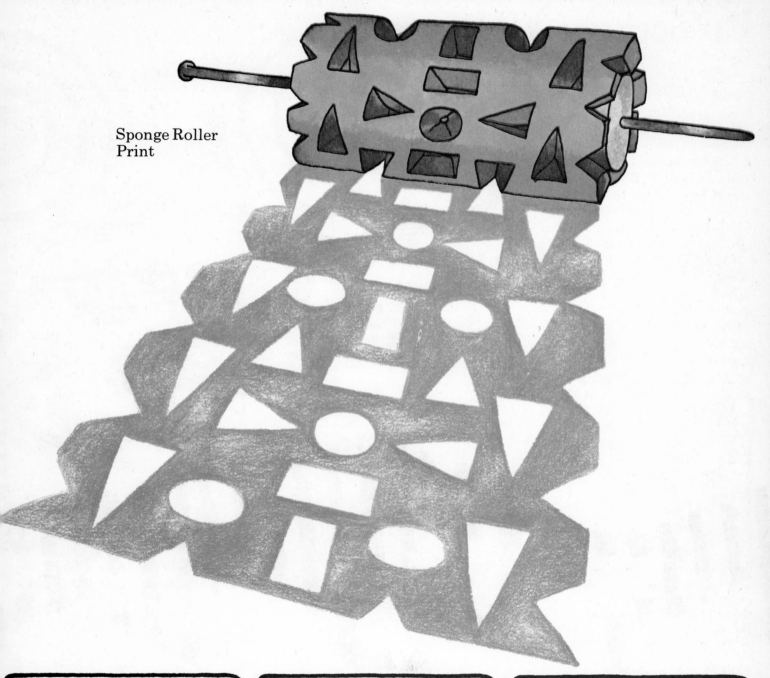

Sponge Roller
Print

1 A Spool Roller

cotton spool

pencil

Cover an empty spool with a thick layer of art eraser or clay. Push a pencil through the holes in the cotton spool.

2

make shapes

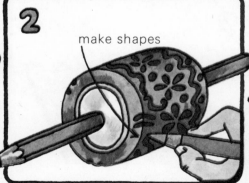

Press different shapes into the art eraser or clay using either end of a pencil. Press hard on the pencil to make deep marks in the art eraser or clay.

3

Roll the spool in paint and push it across the paper. Before using another color, wash the paint off the art eraser or clay with some soap and water.

Printing with Blocks

Make a printing block and use it as many times as you like. Try printing a border or rows of shapes to make a pattern. When you have printed one color, wipe the block with a damp rag and use it again for another color. Remember, when you print a shape, it will be the other way around from the one you cut out.

You will need
small blocks of wood
poster paint
strong all purpose glue
an old plate or a baking tray
sheets of paper to print on
string for string block prints
thick cardboard for cardboard
   blocks
corrugated cardboard for
   stripey block prints
old newspaper
scissors

Card Block Fish

Stripey Block Tigers

Cardboard Block Prints

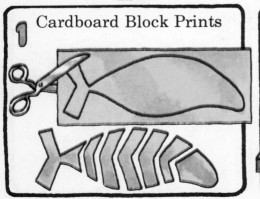

1

2 stick on shapes

3 press

Draw a shape, smaller than the block of wood, on a piece of thick cardboard. Cut out the shape in one piece or cut it into lots of different pieces, like this.

Spread glue over the block of wood. Arrange the shapes on the wood and press them down on the glue. Let the glue dry before starting to print with the block.

Pour some thick paint onto a tray or plate and spread it out evenly. Dip the block onto the paint, making sure the cardboard shapes are well covered with paint.

String Block Snails

draw shape on block

Instead of cardboard shapes, try using a piece of string. Draw a shape or pattern on a small block of wood, like this.

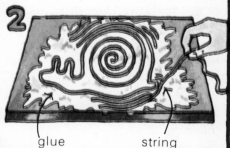

2

glue   string

Cover the block with glue. Put the string on the shape or pattern you have drawn. Leave it to dry and then dip it in some paint to print with it.

4   press hard

Put a sheet of paper on top of some layers of newspaper. Press the block onto the paper. Press hard and evenly on the block, like this to get a good print.

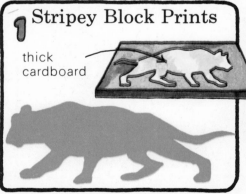

Stripey Block Prints

1   thick cardboard

Cut a shape out of thick cardboard and glue it to a block of wood. Dip the shape in thick, bright paint and make a print with it on a sheet of drawing paper.

2   corrugated cardboard

Cut the same shape out of some corrugated cardboard and glue the flat side to another block of wood. Dip it in a dark paint and press it over the first print.

19

Printing a Cartoon

Cut out this cardboard cartoon man and you can print a whole story with one block. You will need a piece of thick expanded polystyrene (see page 4). When you have made one printing block, you can add more pieces of cardboard. You could give the man a stick or an umbrella to carry.

You will need

a piece of expanded polystyrene, about 1¼ in. thick
thick cardboard, or two pieces of thin cardboard stuck together
some pins
thick poster paint
a plate or old baking tray
sheets of paper
old newspaper
a paintbrush
scissors

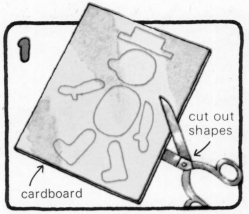

Draw the shape of a cartoon man on a piece of thick cardboard. Cut out the shape in pieces so the arms, legs, head, body and hat are separate pieces.

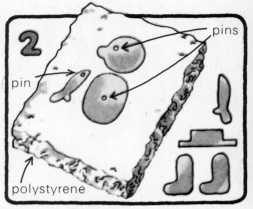

Push a pin through the body and into the polystyrene block. Pin on the arms, legs and head close to the body. Pin the hat near the top of the head.

Put some thick poster paint on the plate or tray and spread it out with a brush. Dip the cardboard shape in the paint, making sure it is well covered with paint.

Press the polystyrene block, paint side down, on a piece of scrap paper. When you can make a good print, put a sheet of paper on newspaper and print the shape.

When you have printed the man standing, try moving his legs apart to make him walk or step forward. Then make a print.

To make him run, move his legs farther apart and tilt his body forward. Then print him again.

To make the man go the other way, take his legs and head off the block. Pull out the pins, turn the shapes over and pin them to the block again.

Charlie Card

When you have made a cartoon block, you can print as many pictures as you like, changing the man a little for each print. Try printing a dog by cutting out a body, four legs, a head and a tail. Pin them onto a separate block. When you have made lots of prints, draw or paint in a path, trees, houses and other things. Make up a story to go with the pictures. We have started a story about Charlie Card and his dog, Mr. McGreedy, and have left it for you to write an end.

One day Charlie Card takes his dog, Mr. McGreedy, for a walk. Mr. McGreedy lags along behind and thinks the walk is very dull.

Suddenly a great gust of wind blows Charlie Card's hat off. Mr. McGreedy watches it whirl away down the road.

Mr. McGreedy thinks this is more fun and chases after the hat. Charlie Card runs after Mr. McGreedy.

Charlie Card watches the hat and does not see a stone in the road. He trips over it and falls flat on his face.

Slowly Charlie Card gets up. He is wet and muddy and his toe hurts. He wishes he had stayed at home.

He brushes himself off and starts to run after his hat and Mr. McGreedy who is a long way away. Now it begins to rain.

Charlie Card has almost caught up with Mr. McGreedy when they come to the bank of a river.

Mr. McGreedy is watching the hat. He does not see the river and over he goes. Charlie Card just manages to grab his tail. Now write the end of the story.

Making Stencils

Cut out a stencil and use the hole or the cut-out shape to print patterns and pictures.

You will need
thin cardboard, brown paper or
   stencil paper
thick poster paint
an old baking tray or plate
a fine sponge
self-adhesive labels
an old toothbrush or a stencil
   brush
a diffuser (see page 4)
a paintbrush
sheets of paper
scissors and old newspaper

1 Cardboard or Paper Stencils

push through

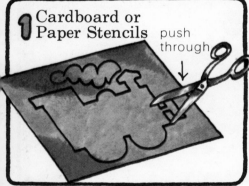

Draw a shape on some thin cardboard or thick paper. Push the scissors through the cardboard and cut neatly around the shape, being careful not to tear the edges.

2

stencil (a)

card cut-out (b)

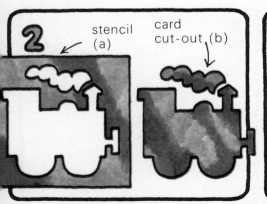

You now have two stencils. One has the shape cut out of it (a), which you can dab paint through. The other is a cut out shape (b), which you can dab paint around.

3

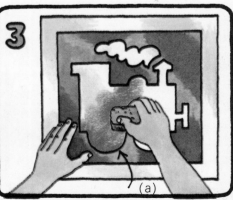

(a)

Hold stencil (a) down on a sheet of paper, being careful not to move it. Dip a fine sponge in poster paint and dab the paint through the stencil, like this.

4

(b)

Take the stencil off and let the paint dry. Put the stencil cut-outs (b) over the colored shapes and dab a different color around the edges, like this.

Use a Toothbrush

newspaper

Put a stencil down on a sheet of paper. Dip an old toothbrush in paint, bend back the bristles with your thumb and splatter paint over the stencil.

Use a Stencil Brush

Dip a stencil brush in paint and dab over or around a stencil. To make the color very bright, let the first coat dry and then dab on another color.

---

1 Label Stencils

Buy different shaped self-adhesive labels from a stationery shop. Stick them on some paper in a shape or pattern. Do not press too hard or the labels will not peel off afterwards.

2

newspaper

Sponge poster paint around the label shape or pattern. Dab the paint as close to the label edges as possible to make a very clear outline.

3

draw around shape

When the paint is dry, peel off the labels very carefully. Draw or paint around the shape or pattern, like this.

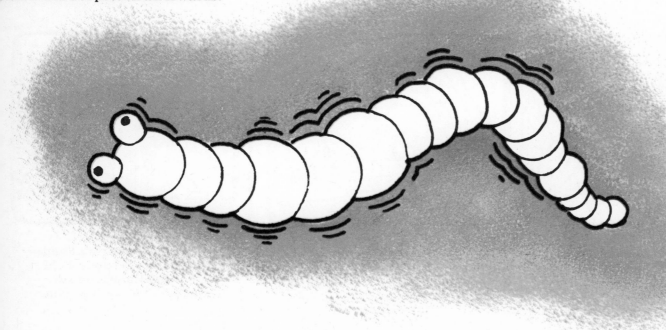

More Stencils

Stencils are quick and easy to make and can be used over and over again. Stencil prints are good for wrapping paper, invitation cards and birthday cards (see page 46). Try printing stencils with dyes and inks on cloth (see pages 38–39).

You will need
sheets of newspaper
a fine sponge
poster paint
sheets of paper for printing on
cardboard stencils (see page 22)
scissors and a pencil
an old plate for mixing paint

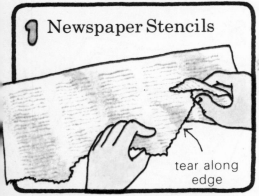

Newspaper Stencils

tear along edge

To make the wavy sea, tear long pieces along the edge of a sheet of newspaper, like this. Tear round, bumpy shapes for the clouds.

cloud shapes

Put the newspaper shapes down on a piece of paper. Dab poster paint around the edges with a fine sponge. Leave the paint to dry.

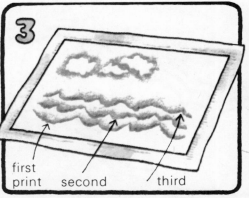

first print   second   third

Put the same newspaper shape down overlapping the first print and sponge paint around the edges. Do this again until you have printed the wavy sea.

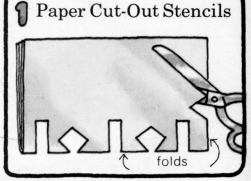

Paper Cut-Out Stencils

folds

Fold a sheet of paper in half, and then in half again. Cut shapes out along the folded edges. Fold the paper in half again and cut more shapes out of the new fold.

Draw this monster, the hills and sun on a piece of cardboard. Cut them out and dab paint through the stencil onto some paper. Then put in the sea and the clouds with newspaper stencils.

Open out the stencil paper. Put it on a sheet of paper and dab different colored paint over the cut-out shapes with a sponge. Take off the stencil.

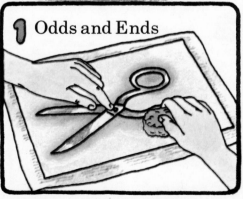

Odds and Ends

You can stencil around lots of different things. Scissors make a good stencil shape. Hold the scissors flat on some paper, like this, and sponge paint around them.

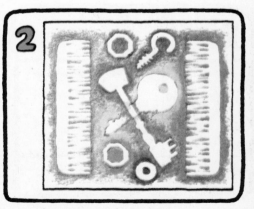

Use other flat things that you can find at home. Try things like keys, combs, hooks, table knives and faucet washers, like this.

Printing Letters

Make these stencil, block and string alphabets to print letters and numbers. Or make up your own letters in any shape and size you like.

You will need
thick paper for the stencil
   alphabet
thick cardboard for the block
   and string alphabets
scissors and some string
a pencil and a ruler
sheets of paper
glue (all purpose)
an old baking tray

Marking Up

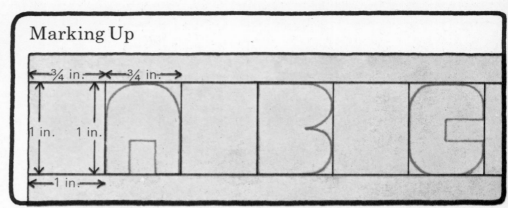

For the stencil letters, use thick paper. For the string and block letters, use thick cardboard. First rule a line on the paper or cardboard.

Rule another line 1 in. below it. Put a ruler on the top line, mark off ¾ in. spaces and rule lines as shown. Draw the letters of the alphabet in every other space.

Stencil Letters

Draw the letters on a sheet of thick paper and cut out each letter. Be careful not to tear the edges of the letters. Use the stencil to print names and words.

String Letters

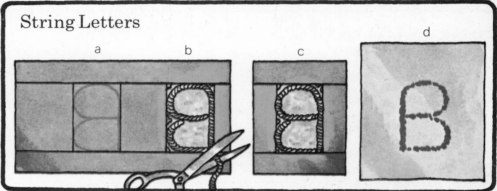

Rule lines and draw a letter (a). Spread on glue and press down the string in the shape of a letter. Cut off the extra string (b).

Cut around the letter to make a small square of cardboard, like this (c). Dip the letter in poster paint and print with it (d).

① Block Letters

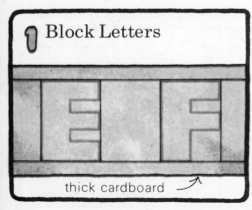

Mark up the alphabet on some thick cardboard and cut out the letters. Put the cut-out letter on another piece of cardboard, draw around it and cut out a second letter.

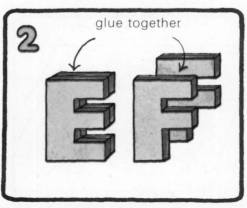

Glue the two letters together, like this, to make a very thick cardboard letter which will print clearly.

Cut out a piece of cardboard a little bigger than the letter. Glue the letter, back to front, onto it. Press the cardboard block in some paint and print with it.

Stencil and Block Alphabet

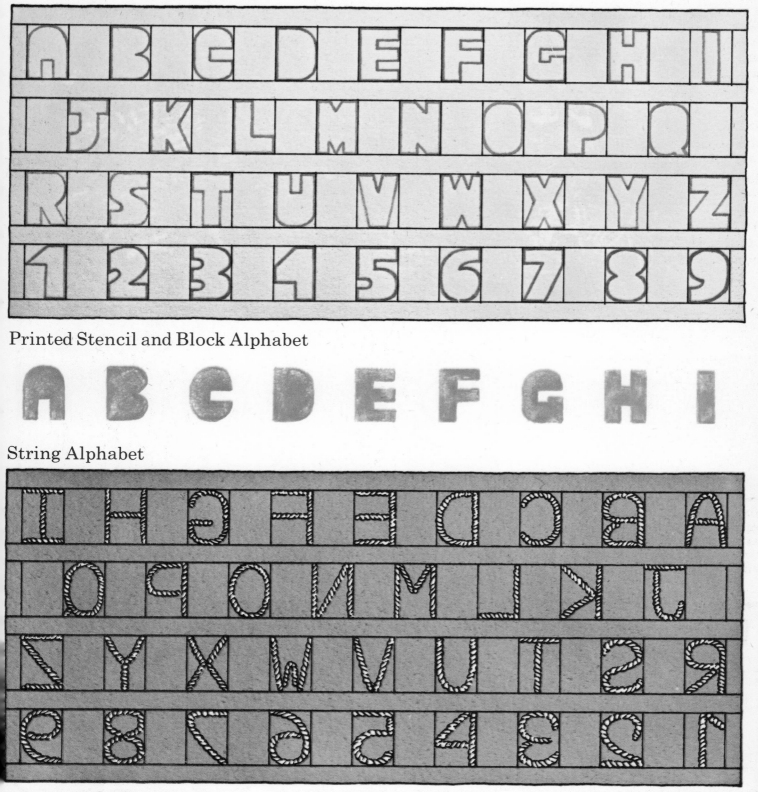

Printed Stencil and Block Alphabet

A B C D E F G H I

String Alphabet

Printed String Alphabet

A B C D E F G H I

Monoprints

These prints are called monoprints because you can never make two prints exactly the same. Before you start, cut out a window mount. It holds the paper just above the paint and makes prints with tidy edges. The paint for monoprints must be sticky and not too wet. If a print has splotches on it, leave the paint on the tray to dry a little before trying again. If there is too little paint on a print, add a few drops of water to the paint and mix it with a brush.

You will need
poster paint or block printing
   paint (see page 4)
an old baking tray or old mirror
a sponge roller (see page 16)
thin cardboard for a window
   mount
a ruler and a pencil
sheets of paper
a paintbrush
scissors

1 One-Color Monoprints

rule lines

Cut some cardboard to fit on the tray or mirror. Put a ruler on one edge of the card and rule a line, like this. Rule lines along the other sides. Cut along the lines.

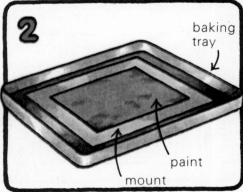

2

baking tray

paint

mount

Spread sticky paint with a roller over the tray or mirror. Put the cardboard mount on the paint. The paint should fill the inside of the mount.

3 draw shape

Put a sheet of paper over the mount. Hold the paper down very gently at one corner, like this. Draw a shape or pattern on the paper.

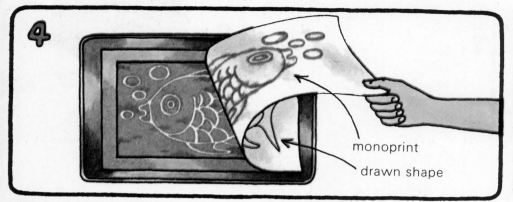

4

monoprint

drawn shape

Lift up one corner of the paper and peel it off the paint. You now have a monoprint on the other side of the piece of paper.

When you are drawing a picture, remember that the monoprint will be the other way around.

5

negative print

Before the paint dries on the tray or mirror, put a new sheet of paper on it and rub it all over with your hand. The print you make like this is called a negative print.

1 Three-Color Prints

first color

Make a monoprint using one color and let it dry. Wash the paint off the tray or mirror and spread on a different color. Put the mount over the paint again.

2

second color

third color

Put the print down on the second color, paint side down. Draw in more parts of the picture or pattern. Lift up the paper and let it dry. Do the same with a third color.

Shading

Put a sheet of paper on the paint and press it lightly with your fingers to get shading or patches of color. Or drag a comb across the paper to make wriggly lines.

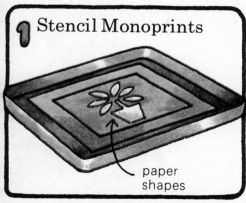

1 Stencil Monoprints

paper shapes

Cut or tear different shapes out of paper and arrange them on the paint. Put a sheet of paper over the shapes and press down on the paper.

2

lift off shapes

Lift up the paper. Pick the paper shapes off the paint very carefully, like this. Put a new piece of paper on the paint and rub over it to make a negative print.

Scrape Prints

scrape lines

Scrape a shape or pattern in the paint with the handle of a paintbrush. Put a piece of paper over the paint and rub all over it to make a print.

Scratch Pictures

Use lots of brightly colored wax crayons to make these scratch prints. Dark colors will not show up on the black paint or ink. Try scratching animal or monster faces and cut them out to make masks.

You will need
colored wax crayons
black poster paint or black
   drawing ink
a white candle
sheets of white paper
a paintbrush

1 Paint on Wax Prints

Draw thick lines with different colored wax crayons on a sheet of paper. Press down hard on the crayons so that you make bands of thick color.

2

black paint or ink

Paint all over the lines with black poster paint or drawing ink. If the wax colors are difficult to cover, brush on two or three coats of black paint or ink.

3

When the paint or ink is dry, scratch it off in a shape or pattern with the handle of a paintbrush to show the wax colors underneath.

Paint on Wax Snake

Black and White Prints

Rub white candle wax on a piece of paper. Cover the wax with lots of coats of black poster paint. Let it dry and then scratch off the black paint in patterns.

Wax on Paint
Monster

Wax on Paint Prints

1

black
paint
or ink

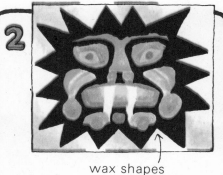

2

wax shapes

3

scratch out
patterns

Paint a shape on a sheet of white paper using black poster paint or black drawing ink.

When it is dry, draw patterns all over the black shape with colored wax crayons. Press hard on the crayons to make thick bands of color, like this.

Use the handle of a paintbrush to scratch black patterns and shapes in the colored crayon.

Paste and Paint Pictures

Try making these bright paste and paint patterns and pictures. Take a print of each one to make another picture. They will all be rough and bumpy.

You will need
white or colored cardboard
  or thick paper
thick paste
poster paint
sheets of paper
a paintbrush

1 Paste and Paint Patterns

Brush three or four stripes of thick paste onto a piece of white or colored cardboard or some thick paper. Brush thick poster paint over the paste.

2

Slide your fingertips or the end of a paintbrush through the paint to make different patterns. If you make a mistake, brush over the pattern and start again.

1 Paste and Paint Prints

Spread paste on some cardboard in the shape of an animal or flower. Brush paint over the paste. Add details by sliding your fingers and brush handle through the paint.

2

To take a print of the picture, lay a sheet of paper on the cardboard, being careful not to smudge the paint.

Rub all over the paper very gently with the side of your hand. Pick up a corner of the paper and peel it off the cardboard.

Wash-Off Pictures

When you have made a wash-off picture, the paper will be very wet. To stop the paper from drying in wrinkles stretch it before you start (see page 5).

You will need
white poster paint
black India ink or colored
    waterproof ink
thick paper
a pencil and a paintbrush
a fine sponge

Draw a picture or a pattern on a sheet of thick paper. Brush white poster paint on the parts of the picture you want to be the color of the paper.

Try dabbing white poster paint on the picture with a fine sponge to make light splotches. Leave the poster paint to dry completely.

Cover the paper and the white poster paint with a layer of black India ink or colored waterproof ink. Leave the ink to dry.

When the ink is dry, hold the picture under running water and gently rub the picture with your hand, like this. The ink that is on top of paint will wash off. Lay the paper down flat to dry.

Wax Patterns and Pictures

Make lots of patterns and pictures with things which have a hard, rough or patterned surface. Put a piece of paper on one and rub over the paper with a wax crayon. Try using leaves, keys, zippers, coins, a flat cheese grater, straw mats, baskets, frosted glass windows, rough wood, a flattened aluminum plate or dish, a comb, a patterned drinking glass, or medals. If you use a white candle, you cannot see the pattern until you brush paint over the paper. The wax shrugs off the paint and the paper is colored only where there is no wax.

You will need
colored wax crayons
a white candle
poster paint
lots of things with a hard, rough
  or patterned surface
sheets of white paper
sheets of colored paper
a pencil
a paintbrush

1 Wax Rubbings

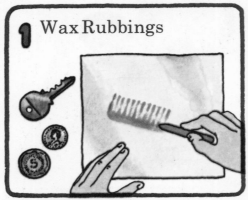

Put a piece of paper over a hard, rough surface. Rub over the paper, pressing down hard, with different colored wax crayons to make a pattern or a picture.

2

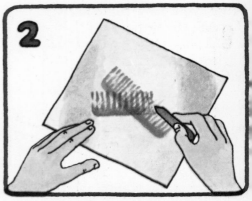

Try moving the paper a little and rub the pattern again with another color. Or turn the paper sideways and rub it with a crayon to make a pattern in a different direction.

1 Wax and Paint Rubbings

Put a piece of paper down on a hard, rough surface. Rub over the paper with a white candle with the wick cut off.

2

Brush some watery poster paint all over the paper to make the pattern show up. Or try using several colors on different parts of the pattern, like this.

3

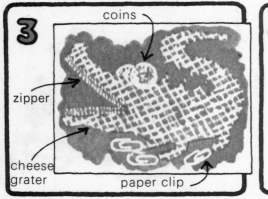

coins

zipper

cheese grater

paper clip

Try putting a sheet of paper on lots of different things, candle rub and then paint the picture.

4

Instead of using a white candle, rub the paper with wax crayons. You can use a different color for each thing you rub. Then brush on thin poster paint.

5

Try rubbing on colored paper. Use light colored crayons on dark paper and dark crayons on light colored paper.

1 Wax Pictures

Sharpen one end of a white candle with a table knife to make a point. Draw a picture or pattern with it on a sheet of paper.

2

If you want to make a picture with lots of things in it, draw it very lightly in pencil first and then go over the pencil lines with the point of the candle.

Brush one color of thin poster paint over the paper or try using several colors. Remember that where you have drawn with the candle it will be white.

Mixing Colors

Red, blue and yellow, black and white paints can be mixed together to make all the colors of the rainbow. Try mixing your own colors, adding a little black or white, to make new colors.

You will need
poster paint
light colored tissue paper
glue
white paper
a string block (see page 19)
a paintbrush
an old plate for mixing colors

Primary and Secondary Colors

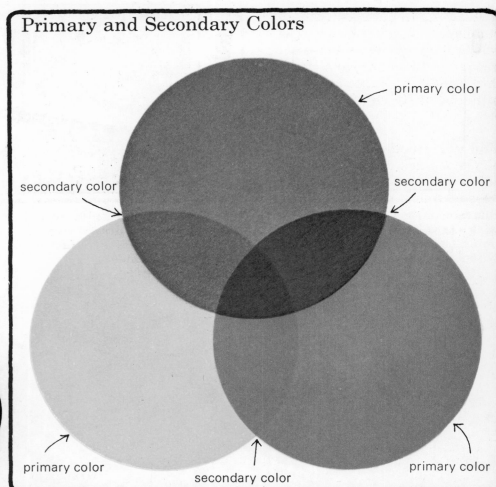

primary color

secondary color

secondary color

primary color

secondary color

primary color

Black and White

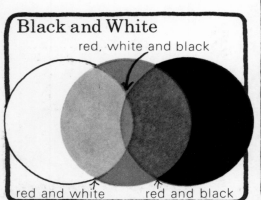

red, white and black

red and white

red and black

To make a color lighter add white. White mixed with red makes pink. To make colors darker, add a little black. Red mixed with black makes dark red.

Red, yellow and blue are called the primary colors. If you mix two primary colors together you get a secondary color. Red and blue make purple. Blue and yellow make green.

Yellow and red make orange. Purple , green and orange are secondary colors. When you mix two colors, mix the lighter color first and then add the darker color.

1 Tissue Pictures

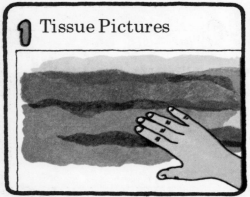

2

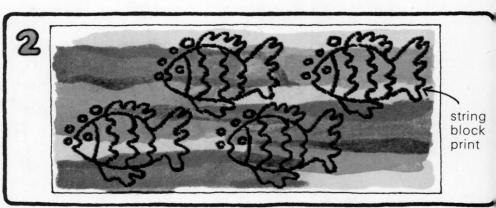

string block print

Tear sheets of light colored tissue paper into strips. Glue the strips onto some white cardboard over-lapping the edges to make new colors, like this.

When the glue on the tissue paper is dry, use a string block and black paint to print shapes or patterns on it, like this.

Instead of using a string block try printing over the tissue paper with a cardboard block (see page 18) or an art eraser or clay block (see page 38).

Overprints

Instead of mixing colors before you use them, try printing one color on top of another to make a new color. To make neat pictures, the cardboard shapes must be printed exactly on top of each other.

You will need
pieces of thick cardboard
poster paint or waterproof inks
scissors and a pencil
sheets of paper
sticky tape loops (see page 43)

Draw a shape on thick cardboard and cut it out. Put the cut-out shape back on the cardboard, draw around it and cut out a second shape. Do this once again.

Stick one shape to a cardboard block with sticky tape loops. Brush ink or paint on the shape and make a print. Before you lift the block off the paper, draw around it.

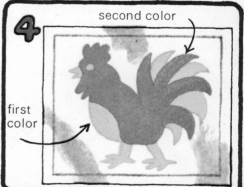

Draw around the shape on the cardboard. Pull the shape off. Cut pieces out of the second cardboard shape and stick it to the block so that it fits inside the pencil marks.

Put a second color on the shape. Fit the block inside the marks on the paper and print over the first color. Cut pieces out of the third shape and print in a new color.

37

Printing on Cloth

Use fabric or textile paint, or waterproof inks to print bright patterns and letters on all sorts of materials, clothes and canvas shoes.

Put down lots of newspaper before you start. If you get paint or ink on any furniture or the floor, wipe it off at once with a rag and lots of water, or it will stain. Practice on a scrap piece of cloth before printing on clothes or material. Make sure they are dry and clean before making a print. Remember to print dark colors on light colored cloth. Light colored paints and inks will not show up on dark material. You can try printing on almost any kind of material but you will get the best results on cotton cloth.

You will need
fabric or textile paint
waterproof inks
pieces of cloth and clothes for
   printing on
art eraser or clay for art
   eraser or clay blocks
cookies for cookie prints
a white candle for wax and dye
   patterns
expanded polystyrene,
   cardboard and pins for
   printing blocks
a long stick or bamboo for wall
   hangings
string
needle and thread
a paintbrush and a pencil
an old baking tray or plate for
   mixing colors
lots of newspaper

1 Art Eraser or Clay Blocks

Shape some art eraser or clay into a square block. Make patterns or shapes in one side by pressing the end of a pencil into the art eraser or clay.

2

Put some ink or paint on the tray or plate. Press the block, pattern side down, onto it and print the pattern on a piece of clean cloth or on old clothes.

Cookie Prints

Use a hard cookie with a pattern on it as a printing block. Brush ink or paint onto one side and then make a print on some material.

Wax and Paint

candle wax

fabric paint

Draw a pattern on a piece of white cloth with a white candle, pressing down very hard. Brush ink or paint over the cloth. It will stay white where the candle lines are.

1 Cardboard Blocks

pin

cardboard shapes

Cut a flower shape out of thick cardboard. Push a pin through the middle and then into the block of thick expanded polystyrene.

2

cardboard block print

Stuff white canvas shoes with newspaper. Brush ink or paint over the cardboard flower and print the shape on the shoes.

T-Shirts

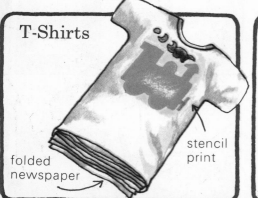

folded newspaper

stencil print

Put folded newspaper inside a T-shirt to stop the paint going through to the other side. Use a stencil to print a pattern or your name in bright ink or paint.

1 Wall Hangings

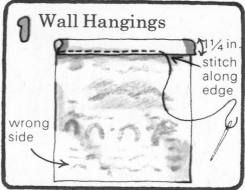

1¼ in.
stitch along edge

wrong side

Print a picture in paint or ink on a large white cloth. A piece of old sheet is good for this. Fold over about 1¼ in. at the top and stitch the edge down, like this.

2

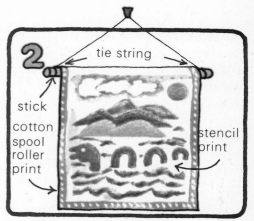

tie string

stick
cotton spool roller print

stencil print

Push a long stick or bamboo through the stitched pocket. Tie the ends of a piece of string to the stick or bamboo and hang the picture up.

Blue Jeans

newspaper

string block patch

Print ink or paint patterns on the pockets of light blue jeans or print patches and sew them on. Remember to put newspaper in the pockets before you begin.

Scarves and Handkerchiefs

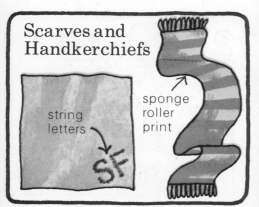

string letters

sponge roller print

Try printing stenciled names or initials on handkerchiefs to make presents. Or use a sponge roller to print stripes on a scarf.

Poster Factory

Several people working together can set up a production line and produce lots of good posters quickly. Each person should have a particular job to do. Lay out everything carefully so that they have the tools they need. Stack newspaper on the work tables. Hang the posters up to dry after each step.

First make the poster borders using a light color. Then print patterns on top of the border in a darker or brighter color. Use the stencil, block or string alphabets on page 26 for the lettering on the posters.

You will need
paper and poster paint
a sponge roller (see page 16) or a fine sponge
thick paper for the stencils
a spool roller (see page 17)
an art eraser or clay block (see page 38)
a string block (see page 19)
thick cardboard and some string
a baking tray and some scissors
strong all purpose glue
lots of newspaper and rags for keeping clean

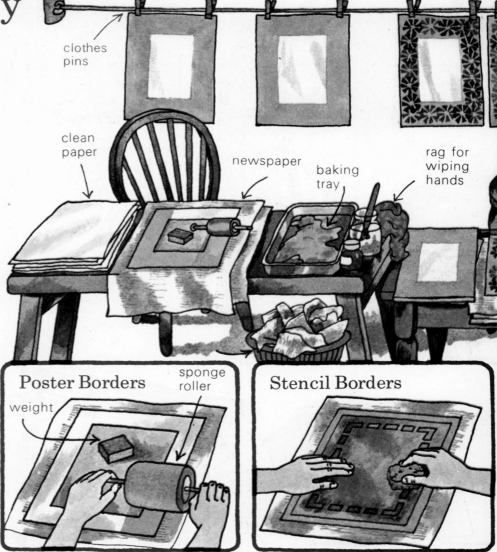

clothes pins

clean paper

newspaper

baking tray

rag for wiping hands

Poster Borders

sponge roller

weight

Lay a neat rectangle of thick paper in the middle of the poster. Roll or dab paint around the edges, like this. Lift up the rectangle and let the paint dry.

Stencil Borders

Cut out a stencil (see pages 22 and 24). Lay it down over the border and dab a second color through it.

One-Block Posters

Instead of using lots of different prints on a poster, try making a one block poster. Cut a piece of cardboard the same size as the poster paper.

Mark up the cardboard (see page 26) and glue string letters onto it. Glue a string pattern around the edges. Roll paint over the string letters and print with it.

String Block Borders

Try making an oblong poster, like this, and printing patterns around the poster border with a string block or a cardboard block.

art eraser
or clay

plate
for paint

stencil
letters

baking tray

sponge

delivery
wagon

Spool Borders

Make a pattern on a spool roller to go with what the poster is advertising. This poster could be advertising a play or a puppet show.

Art Eraser or Clay Block Borders

An art eraser or clay block is easy to make (see page 38) and you can print patterns quickly with it. Use lots of different colors and try overlapping the pattern, like this.

When you are making posters remember to use thick paper which will not crumple or wrinkle. Print them with large, simple patterns in bright colors.

Instead of printing poster borders, try gluing on strips of colored paper. If you hang the posters outdoors, put them in large plastic bags to keep them dry.

Putting on an Exhibition

When you have printed lots of pictures and patterns, try putting on an exhibition. Frame or mount your pictures on colored cardboard first. Here are some ideas on how and where to hang your pictures if you have an outdoor show. For an indoor show, tie string to points in a room and hang the pictures from the string. Send printed invitation cards telling everyone where to come, at what time and whether it will cost them anything. Make posters to advertise the exhibition.

You will need
printed pictures
sheets of colored cardboard
   for the frames
a ruler
a pencil
sticky tape
string
an old sheet
scissors
clothes pins, paper clips or pins
posters (see pages 40-41)
invitation cards (see page 46)

1. Colored Cardboard Mounts

glue on

Dab a little glue on the four corners of the back of a picture. Put the picture down on a sheet of colored cardboard, like this, and rub all over it with your hand.

2.

rule lines

Put a ruler on the edge of one of the sides of the picture and rule a line like this. Do the same with the other three sides of the picture.

3.

cut along lines

Cut along the four ruled lines with scissors. Put sticky tape loops on the four corners of the back of the cardboard to hang the picture up.

Sticky Tape Loops

sticky side out

Curl a small piece of tape, the sticky side outside, into a loop and stick the ends together. Put a loop in each corner of a picture to hang it up.

String Loops

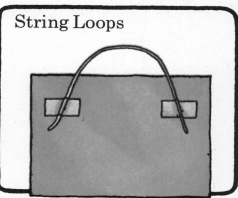

Tape a piece of string to the cardboard on the back of a picture, like this. Hang the picture from the middle of the string.

How to Hang Pictures

Think how tall the people you are inviting to your exhibition are and hang your pictures so that they are on a level with the people's eyes.

Ask a friend to hold the picture while you stand back to see if it is in the right position. With two rows of pictures, hang one just above eye level and one just below.

1 Cardboard Window Frames

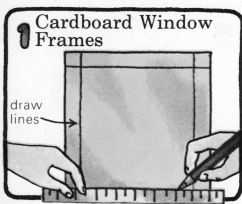

draw lines

To make a window frame, cut a piece of colored cardboard the same size as the picture. Put a ruler on the edges of the cardboard and draw four pencil lines, like this.

2

cut

Cut out the center of the cardboard by pushing one blade of the scissors through the middle of the cardboard. Cut to one corner and then along the lines you have drawn.

3

picture in center

glue on frame

Put a little glue on the four corners of the back of the frame. Place the frame on top of the picture and press down.

Things to Make

When you have lots of prints, you can make your own folders to keep them in. Decorate the outsides with roller or stencil prints, or glue on your own printed paper. Try making your own envelopes for the invitation or birthday cards you have printed. If you want a lot of envelopes, cut out one and use it as a pattern. Put it down on a sheet of paper and draw around it. Fold it up and glue it in the same way as the first one. Use the pattern to make as many envelopes as you need.

Make your own wrapping paper by coloring white tissue paper. You can use as many colors as you like and fold the paper in different ways to make lots of different patterns.

For the folders you will need
large sheets of cardboard
a ruler and a pencil
a stapler or needle and thread
scissors
a piece of ribbon or string

For the envelopes you will need
sheets of paper
scissors and glue
a ruler and a pencil

For the wrapping paper you will need
sheets of white tissue paper
inks or water color paint
old bowls
a paintbrush
old newspaper

1 Big Pocket Folder

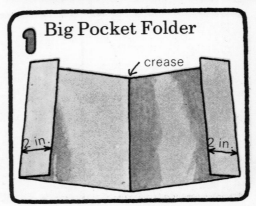

Measure a strip about 2 in. wide at each end of the cardboard. Fold the strips over. Put the edges together and crease the cardboard down the middle.

2

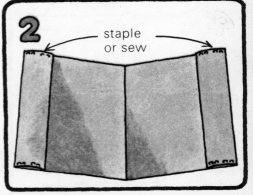

Staple the two flaps at the top and bottom or sew them with a needle and thread. Keep your pictures and prints under each flap.

1 Binder Folder

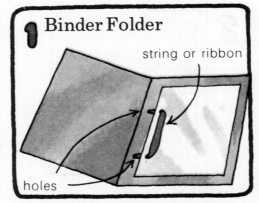

Fold a piece of cardboard in half. Make two holes near the fold and two holes in some paper. Push string or ribbon through the holes, like this, and tie it on the outside.

2

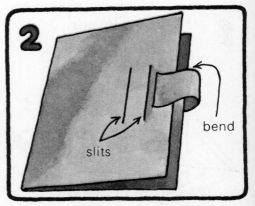

To keep the folder closed, glue a strip of cardboard to one side of the folder. Bend the strip over and cut two slits, like this in the folder. Push the strip through the slits.

1 Making an Envelope

Put the card for which you want to make an envelope down on the bottom edge of a sheet of paper and about ¼ in. from the side, like this.

2

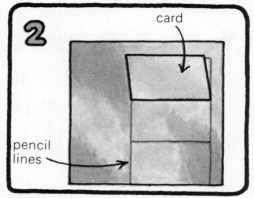

card

pencil lines

Draw a pencil line around the card. Put the card on the top pencil line and draw around the card again. Draw a third box in the same way.

3

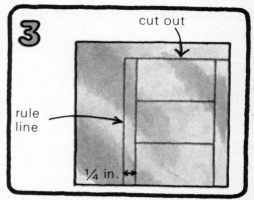

cut out

rule line

¼ in.

Rule a line about ¼ in. from the left hand side of the boxes. Now cut along the outside red lines.

4

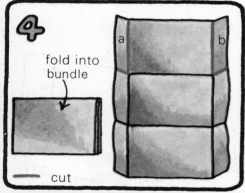

fold into bundle

a   b

cut

Fold the paper along the lines. Unfold the paper and cut off the two pieces (a) and (b).

5

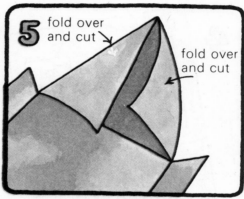

fold over and cut

fold over and cut

Fold over both sides of the top box, like this. Then cut along the fold lines to make a triangle. Round off the point.

6

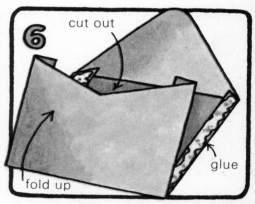

cut out

glue

fold up

Cut a small triangle out of the bottom edge, like this. Glue the side flaps and fold the bottom box over the middle one. Press down the edges.

1 Wrapping Paper

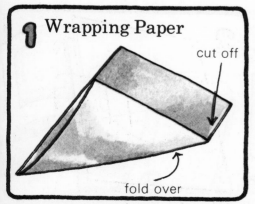

cut off

fold over

Make a sheet of tissue paper into a square by folding a short edge across to a long edge, like this. Cut off the remaining strip.

2

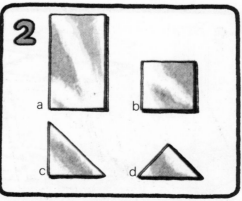

a   b

c   d

Fold the square in half and in half again. Then fold it into a triangle and fold it again.

3

Put some paint into the bowls and stir in a little water. Dip in the edges and corners of the folded paper. Press it very hard between newspaper. Unfold and leave to dry.

More Things to Make

Use your prints to decorate this big calendar. When it is finished, hang it on a wall and move the cardboard day window every day. At the end of the month, change the month window.

You will need
a large sheet of cardboard, about 20 in. long and 8 in. wide
a strip of thick paper, about 12 in. long and 1½ in. wide
2 strips of thick paper, about 4 in. long and 1½ in. wide
2 pieces of cardboard, about 2½ in. square
glue and scissors

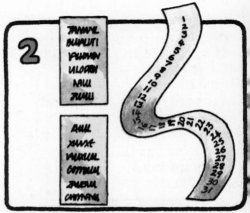

1 Decorate the large piece of cardboard with roller prints and stencils (see pages 16, 22, 24). Or glue a collection of your prints and pictures to it.

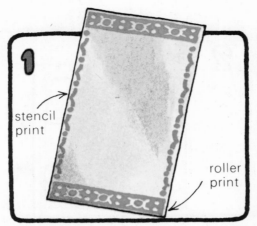

2 Leaving spaces at the top, write the months of the year down the two short pieces of paper. Write or print 1 to 31 on the long paper for the days of the month.

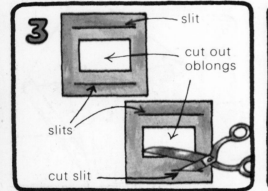

3 Cut out small squares in the center of each piece of square cardboard. Cut slits, about 1½-2 in. long, above and below the cut-out squares.

4 Glue the top ends of the month strips to the top end of the sheet of cardboard. Glue the top end of the day strip below them.

5 Push the month strip through the slits in one square, like this. Move it until you can see the right month in the window. Push on the day strip in the same way.

Using Your Prints

When you have made lots of prints you can use them in all sorts of ways. Cut out small prints and glue them to folded pieces of cardboard to make greeting cards.

Use large roller prints for book covers and wrapping paper for presents. Cover boxes by cutting out pieces for the four sides, the top and bottom and gluing them on.

Cut small roller prints into strips to make book marks. Glue a piece of paper in the middle of a print to make book plates. Write on it "This book belongs to . . ."

Party Prints

Before you have a party, you can make lots of things for it. Start the day before so that the paint and ink have time to dry.

You will need

white paper cups, plates and
   napkins
sheets of paper, about 16 in. long
   and 12 in. wide
waterproof inks
poster paint
an art eraser or clay roller
   (see page 17)
stencils (see pages 22 and 24)
string or stencil letters (see
   pages 26-27)
a pencil and scissors
a sponge and glue

Paper Plates

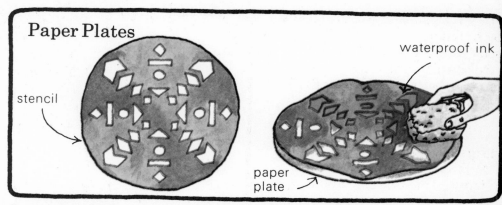

Put a paper plate down on a piece of stencil paper and draw around it. Cut out the circle and fold it up several times. Cut pieces out of the folds to make a stencil.

Unfold the stencil and put it down on a paper plate. Use waterproof inks and a sponge to print the stencil in different colors on the plate, like this.

Paper Hats

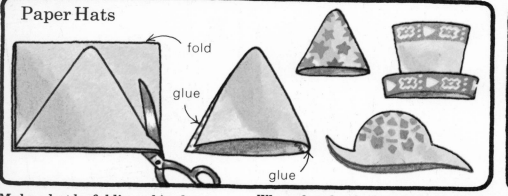

Make a hat by folding a big sheet of paper in half. Cut out a hat shape and glue the two pieces together along the top edges. Try cutting out different shapes.

When the glue is dry, decorate both sides of the hats with art eraser or clay roller prints or stencil prints in several different colors of poster paint, like this.

Paper Cups

Cut a small pattern in a stencil. Wrap it around the outside of a paper cup and use waterproof inks and a sponge to print a pattern.

Paper Napkins

Fold napkins into small squares or triangles. Dip corners or edges in waterproof inks. Press the napkins between newspaper. Unfold and hang up to dry.

Paper Mats

Fold the large sheets of paper in half and cut along the folds. Decorate the edges with art eraser or clay roller prints

Use string or stencil letters to print on the mats the name of each friend coming to the party. Put the mats on the table so that they will know where to sit.